MW01008693

Peter F. Copeland

ANTIQUE AIRPLANES

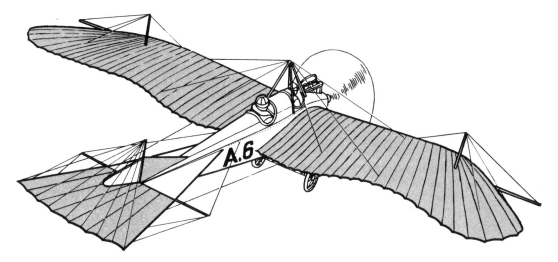

Coloring Book

Dover Publications, Inc.
New York

To Terezia Takacs

Published in Canada by General Publishing Company, Ltd.,
30 Lesmill Road, Don Mills, Toronto, Ontario.
Published in the United Kingdom by Constable and Company, Ltd., 10 Orange Street, London WC 2.

Antique Airplanes Coloring Book is a new work, first published by Dover Publications, Inc., in 1975.

International Standard Book Number: 0-486-21524-5

Manufactured in the United States of America
Dover Publications, Inc.
180 Varick Street
New York, N.Y. 10014

Foreword

The development of powered aircraft represents the most revolutionary advance in the evolution of human transportation in the entire history of man's life on earth.

In the course of one man's life span, the science of aviation has moved from Kitty Hawk to the stars, from frail wooden-sparred, linen-covered kites with tiny gasoline engines to giant rockets exploring the moon and the planets.

This book deals with aero history from the Wright Flyer of 1903, through World War II, into the dawn of the jet and the rocket age.

Model makers and aviation history buffs have always been fascinated with the color schemes of historic airplanes. From the crazy-quilt camouflage of the two World Wars, through the garish stripes and patterns of the early barnstormers and air racers, to the brilliant hues of modern jet airliners, the airplane has presented a colorful picture throughout its history.

The colors of the airplanes given in the captions and shown on the covers are taken from written descriptions, contemporary illustrations and aero history publications, and are historically accurate.

Many of the types of airplanes shown here are on display in museums throughout the world. Some of the planes included in this book will be dramatically displayed at the new National Air and Space Museum of the Smithsonian Institution, which is scheduled to open in Washington, D.C., on July 4, 1976.

Peter F. Copeland
Chief of Illustration Department
NASM, Smithsonian Institution

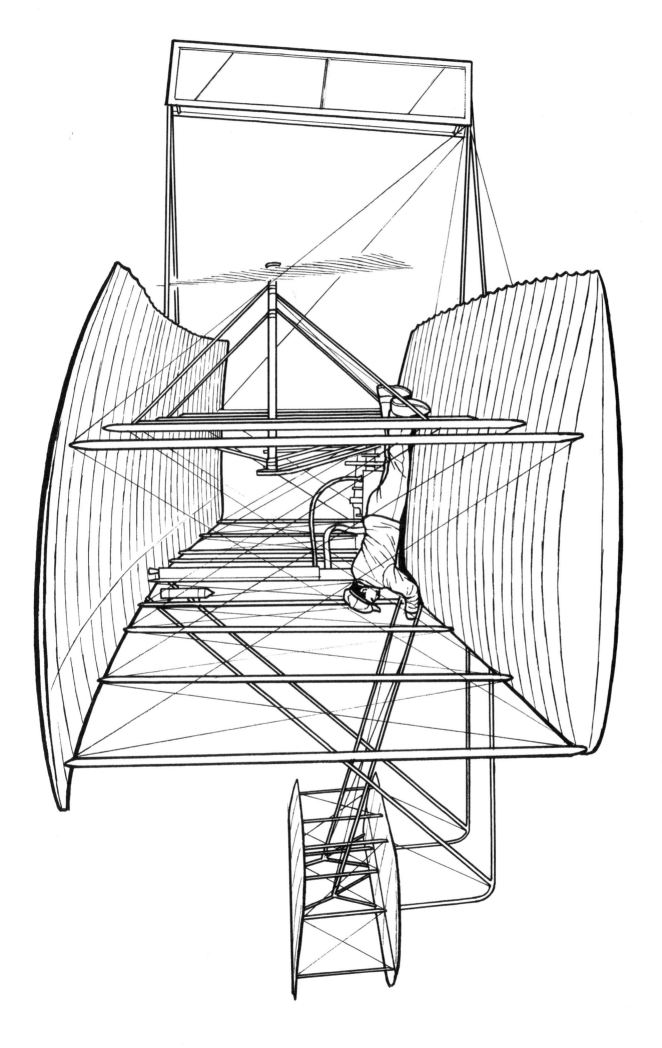

1. **The Wright Flyer,** in which Orville Wright made the first successful powered flight, Dec. 17, 1903. Aircraft was natural unbleached linen color (pale yellowish buff or tan) throughout. Struts were a natural wood color. Wingspan 40'4".

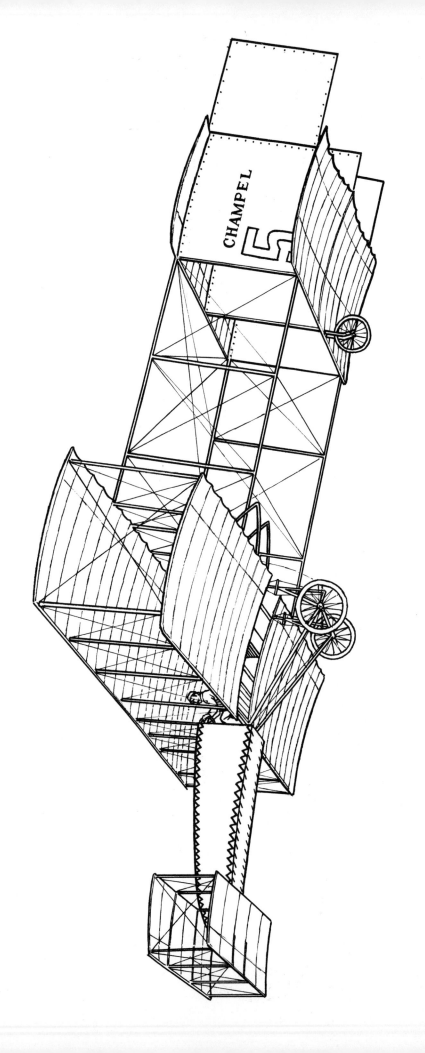

2. Voisin Standard Biplane, 1907. An early French biplane which first flew in March 1907. Aircraft was natural unbleached cotton color (light brown) throughout. Airframe and struts were a natural wood color. Number 5 on tail was painted red. Wingspan 32'10".

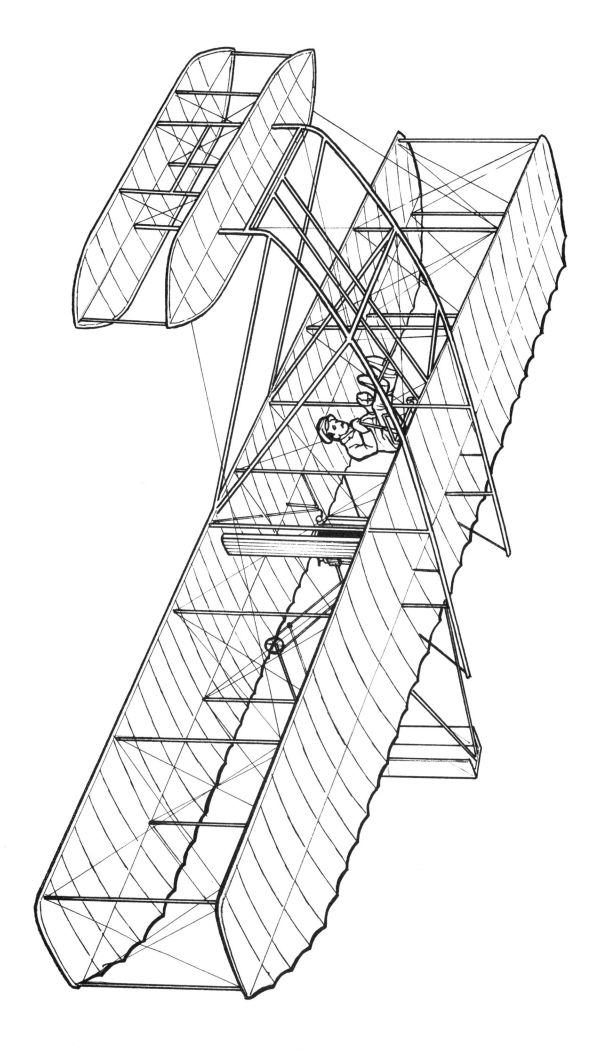

3. **Wright Military Flyer.** Tested for the U.S. Army in July 1909 and later known as Signal Corps No. 1. This aircraft was colored the same as the first Wright Flyer. Wingspan 36'6".

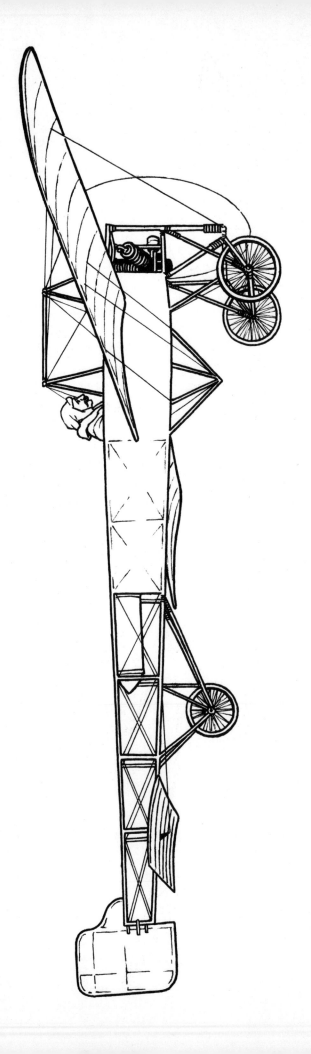

4. **Blériot Type XI.** The first aircraft to fly across the English Channel, piloted by Louis Blériot, July 25, 1909. Aircraft had pale yellow fuselage, pale brown wings and tail. Struts natural wood color. Wingspan 25'6".

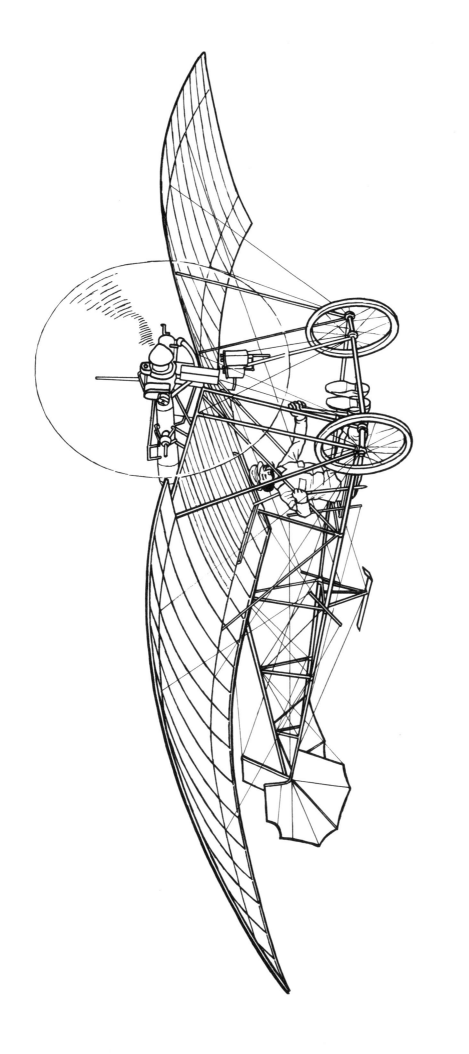

5. Santos-Dumont Demoiselle, 1909. Considered by many to be the first really successful light airplane. Built in France by Brazilian aero pioneer Alberto Santos-Dumont. Aircraft colored pale blue-grey throughout. Airframe and struts natural wood color. Wingspan 16′8″.

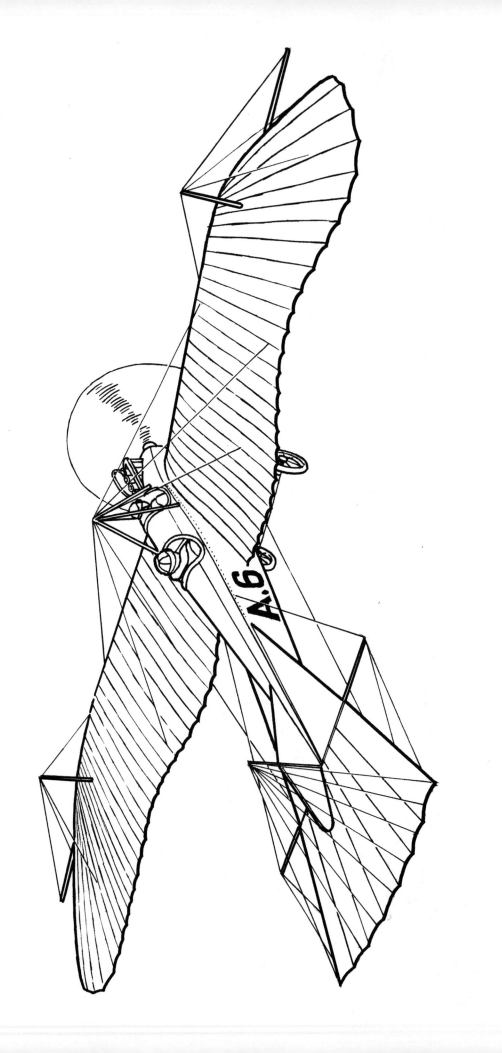

6. Etrich Taube Monoplane, 1911. Designed by Austrian Dr. Igo Etrich, and popularly adopted by the German military at the outset of World War I. Aircraft had pale brown fuselage and wings and yellow tail. Wingspan 47'.

7. Deperdussin Monoplane Racer, 1912. An outstanding, speedy aircraft, the Deperdussin racer was years ahead of its time. Winner of the Gordon Bennett Trophy at Rheims in 1913. Aircraft was colored medium-brown throughout, with pale buff wheels. Wingspan 23′.

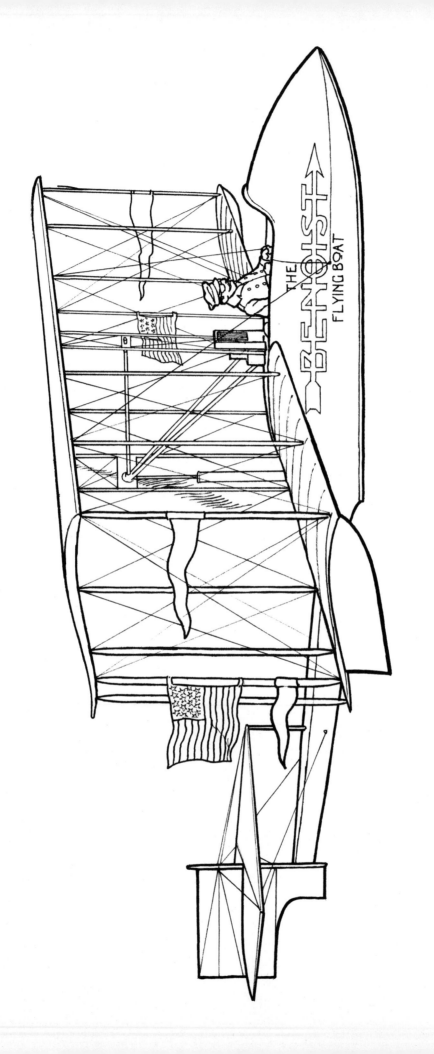

THE BENOIST →
FLYING BOAT

8. **Benoist Flying Boat, 1913.** This aircraft inaugurated the first scheduled airline service in the world, from St. Petersburg to Tampa, Florida, on Jan. 1, 1914. Aircraft was colored medium blue-grey throughout, with white lettering on the nose and red pennants on the leading edge wing struts. Wingspan 49'9".

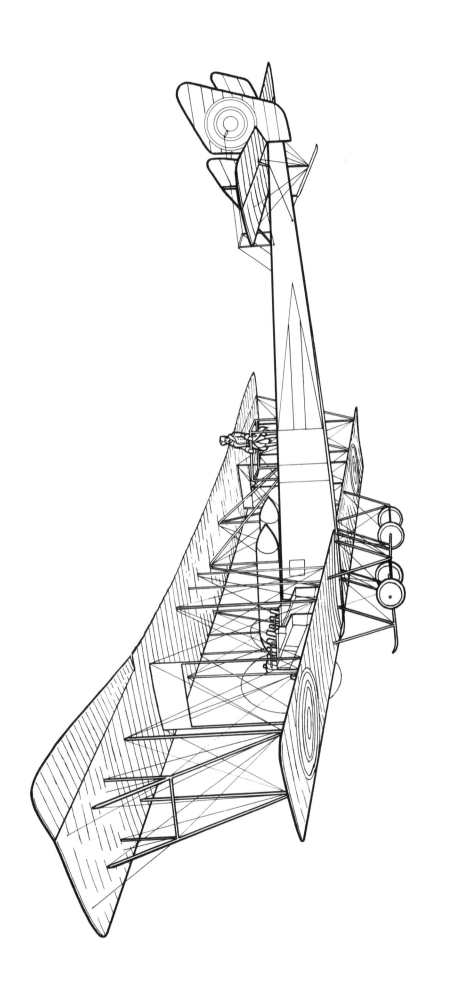

9. Sikorsky "Ilia Mourometz," 1913–1914. The world's first giant airplane. Adopted for use by the Russian Army and Navy at the outbreak of World War I. Aircraft was dark brown from nose to behind the wings. Rear of fuselage was pale grey, pennant painted on fuselage was colored (stripes, top to bottom) white, blue and red. Wings were buff colored and tail was pale grey. Struts were natural wood color. Roundels (Russian insignias on wings and tail) were (outer to inner) white, red, white, blue, white. Wingspan 91'10".

10. B.E.2 A, 1914. A British two-seat observation plane used early in World War I. Airplane was unarmed, but crew members often carried rifles or pistols with which to fire on German airplanes. Aircraft colored pale buff throughout, with struts of natural wood color. Union jack on tail had a dark blue background. Propeller was also natural wood color. Wingspan 35'.

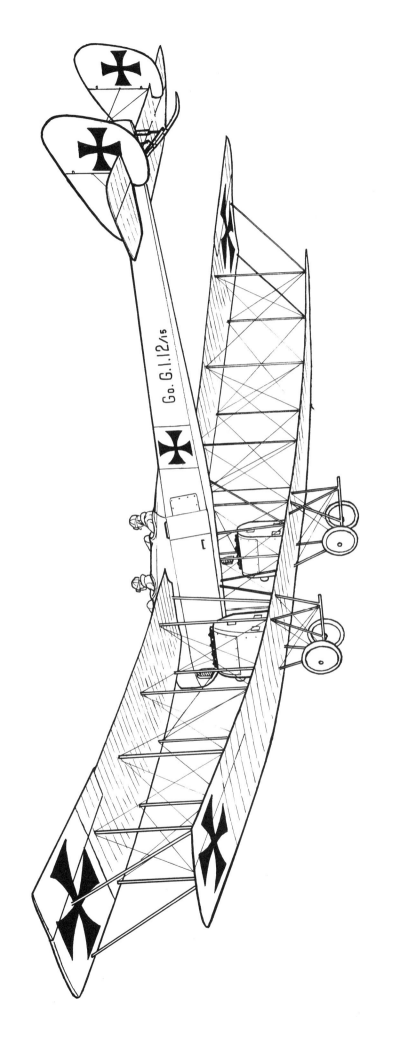

11. **Gotha G-I, 1914–1915.** Early German bombing plane and fore-runner of later Gotha types that bombed London later in World War I. Engines and nose to rear of wings colored pale grey. Remainder of fuselage and vertical tail fin, brown. Box enclosing cross on fuselage, white. Rudder white. Wings brown, with white boxes around crosses. Wingspan 65'6".

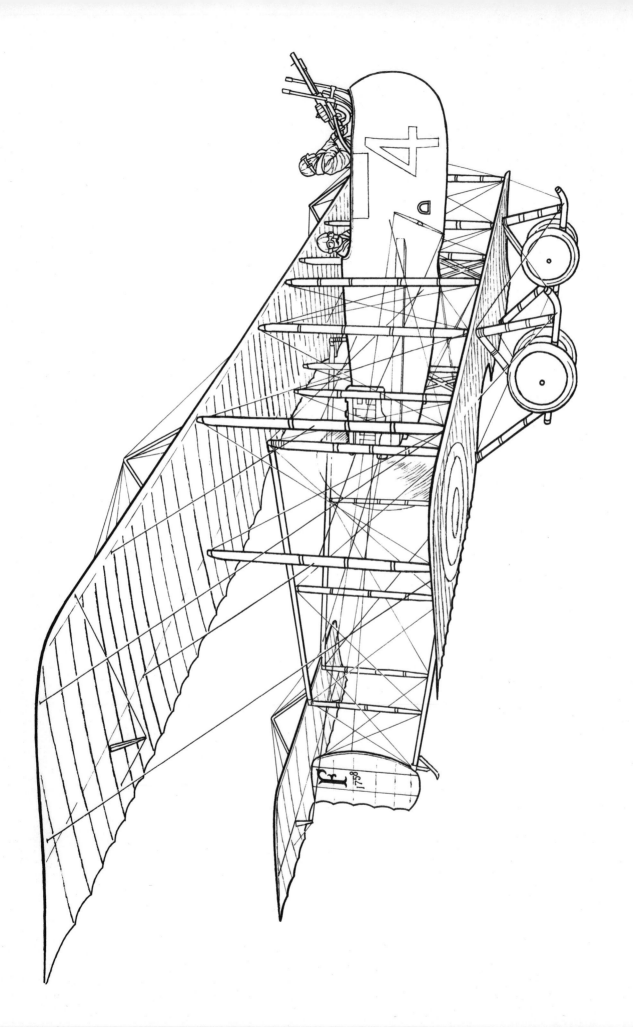

12. Farman Type 40, 1916. A French pusher-type (propeller behind wing) two-seat observation plane, also used by the Belgian air force in World War I. Aircraft had grey-green fuselage and silver-grey wings and horizontal tail section. Rudder was striped (front to rear) red, yellow, black. Wing roundels (Belgian national insignia) were (outer to inner) red, yellow, black. Struts were natural wood. Wingspan 72'.

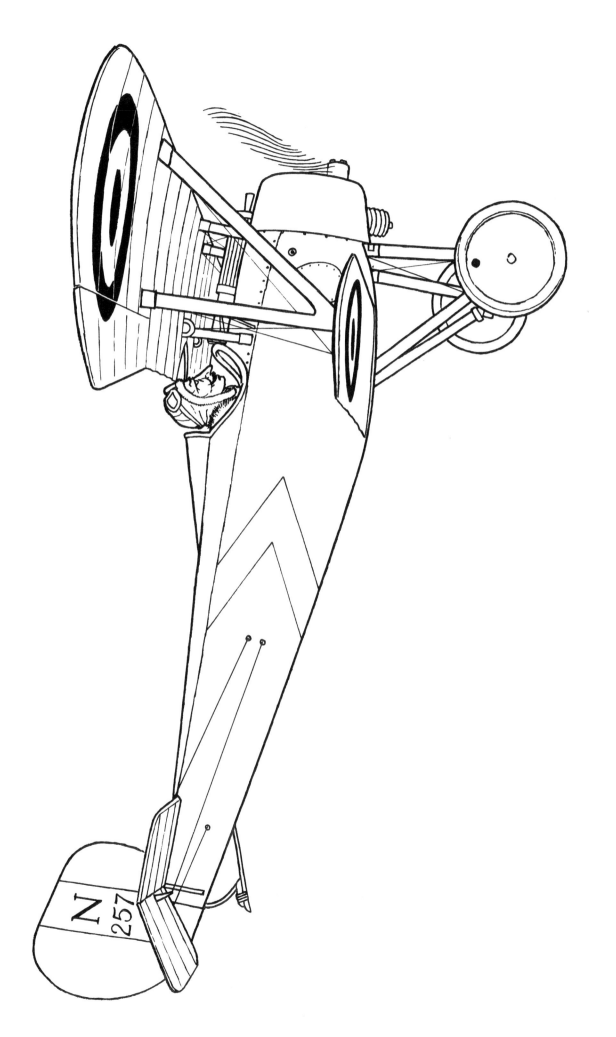

13. Nieuport 17 Scout, 1917. A light maneuverable French fighting scout, this type of craft was flown by the American Volunteers of the Lafayette Escadrille. Aircraft was colored pale silver-grey throughout. Struts of natural wood. Rudder (front to back) blue, white, red. Chevron on fuselage (pilot's personal marking) red. Wingspan 26′.

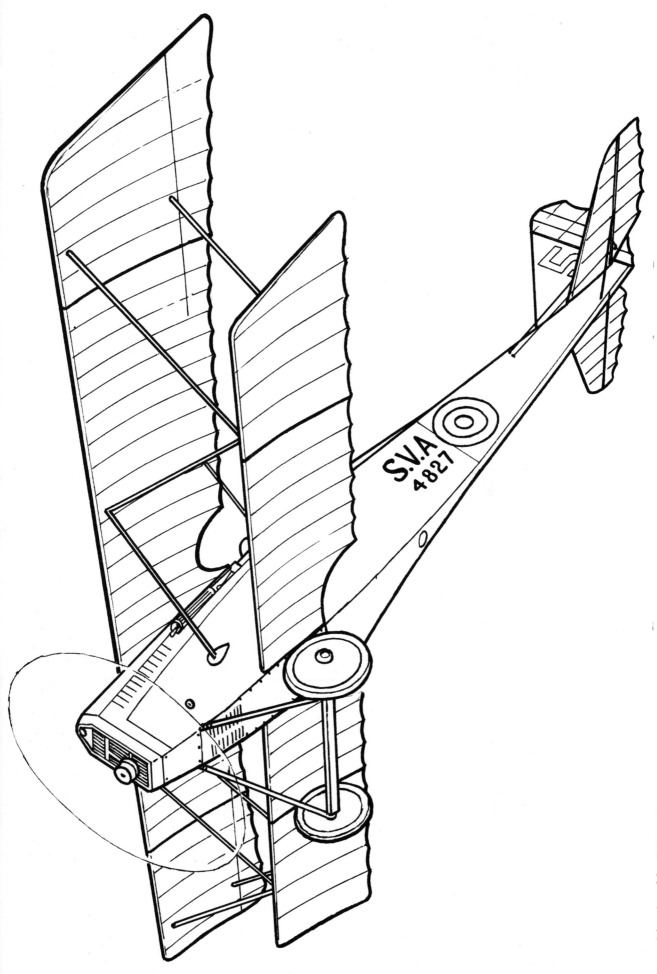

14. Ansaldo S.V.A. Scout, 1917. An Italian fighting scout, the Ansaldo S.V.A. served in World War I and was used as an air racer after the war. Aircraft had greenish-brown fuselage and vertical fin, with buff wings and horizontal tail section. Struts were dark brown. Roundel (Italian national insignia) on fuselage was (outer to inner) green, white, red. Wing tips of upper and lower wings were red. Rudder was (front to rear) red, white, green. Upper portion of nose was pale grey. Number 5 on tail was red. Wingspan 29′8″.

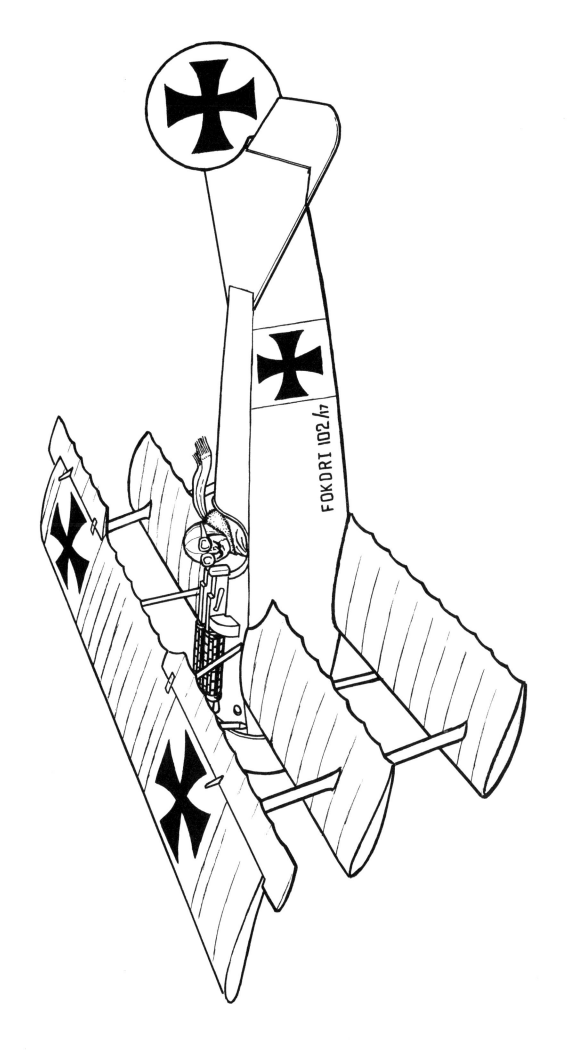

15. Fokker DR-1 Triplane, 1917–1918. Used by the Richthofen Flying Circus of Germany and flown by Richthofen himself at the time of his death, this triplane fighter was designed by the Dutchman Anthony Fokker. Aircraft had a red nose and was colored throughout in a streaky brown and green camouflage. The crosses were in white boxes and the rudder was white. Wingspan 23'7".

FOKDRI 102/17

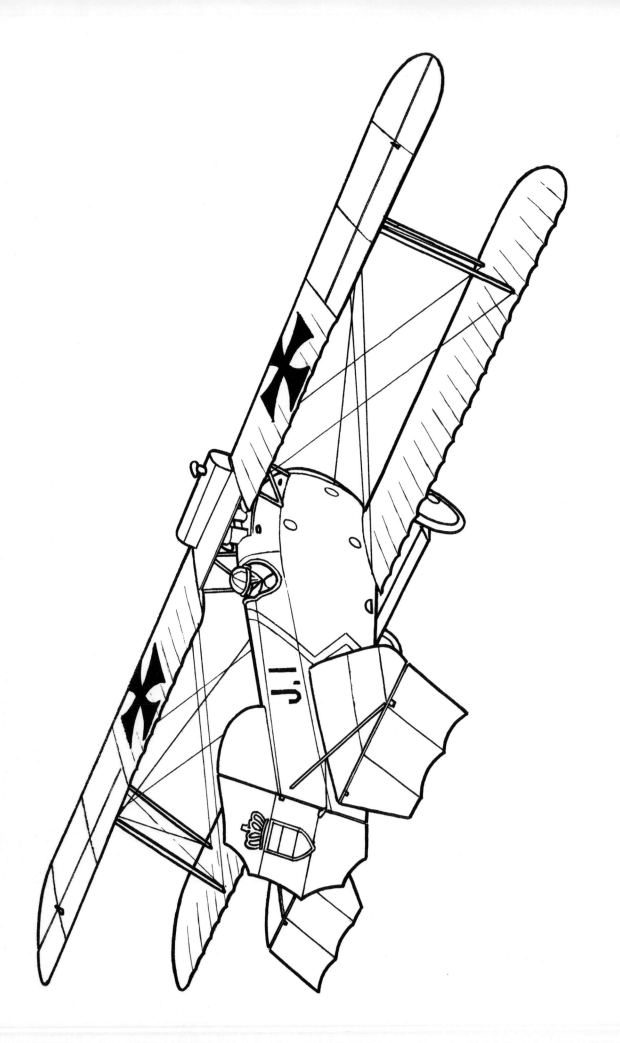

16. Phönix Scout, 1918. Employed as a fighter plane by the Austro-Hungarian Army and Navy during World War I, the Phönix Scout fought mainly on the Italian front. Shown in the colors of the Austro-Hungarian Navy, the aircraft has a dark brown fuselage. The stripe on the fuselage is white. The wings have red-white-red-striped upper wing tips, the inner wing portion and the lower wings are yellow-brown. The horizontal tail section, and the fin and rudder, are striped red, white, red. Wingspan 33'6".

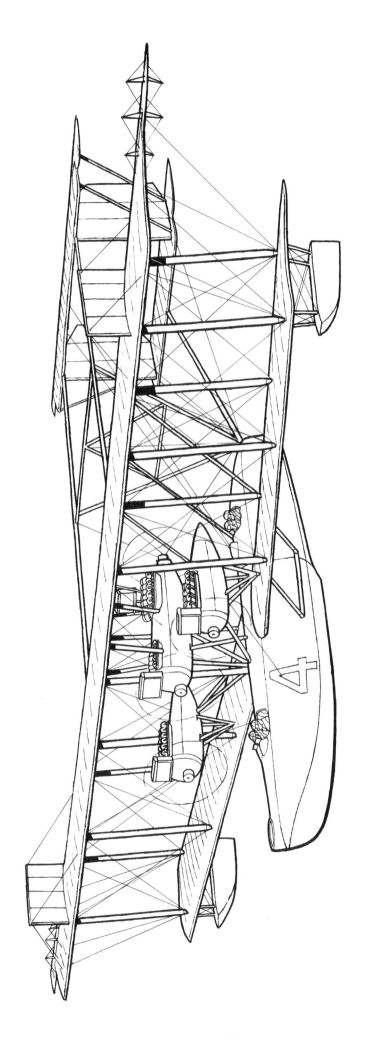

17. NC-4, 1919. This airplane, with a U.S. Navy crew, was the first to cross the Atlantic, in May 1919. The veteran of this flight is now in the collection of the Smithsonian Institution in Washington, D.C. Aircraft had grey-blue fuselage and wingtip floats, silver-grey engines, and pale buff-yellow wings. The rudders were (front to rear) red, white, blue. Struts were light grey. White number 4 on fuselage. Wing-span 126′.

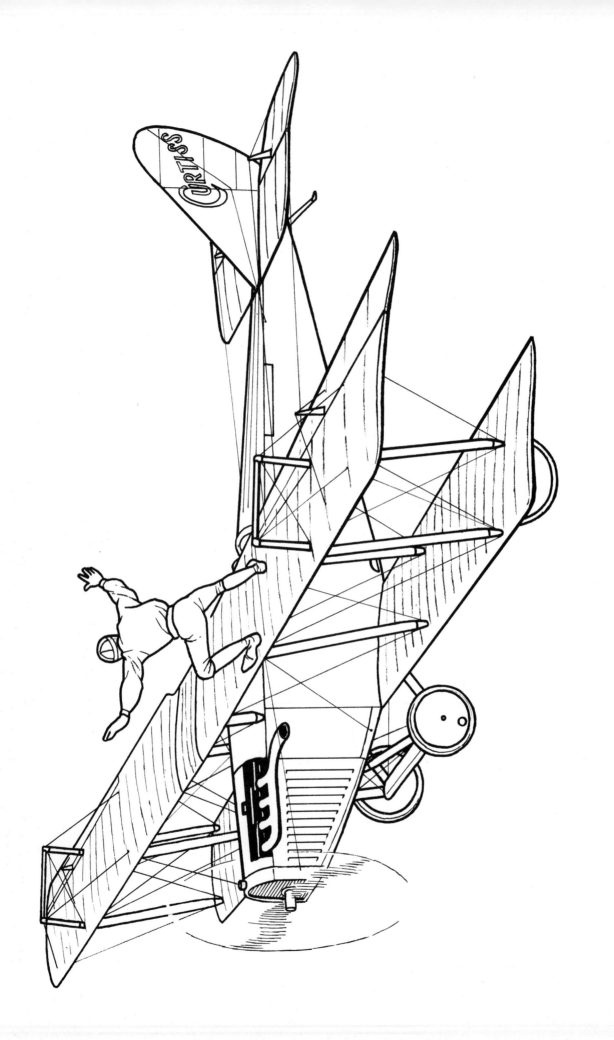

18. Curtiss JN-4 "Jenny," 1916–1926. Originally a two-seat trainer used by the U.S. and Canadian armies in World War I, the "Jenny" had a long life after the war, being especially popular with barnstorming pilots in the 1920s. Aircraft colored bright blue throughout. Wheels, struts and maker's name on tail were white. Wingspan 43'7".

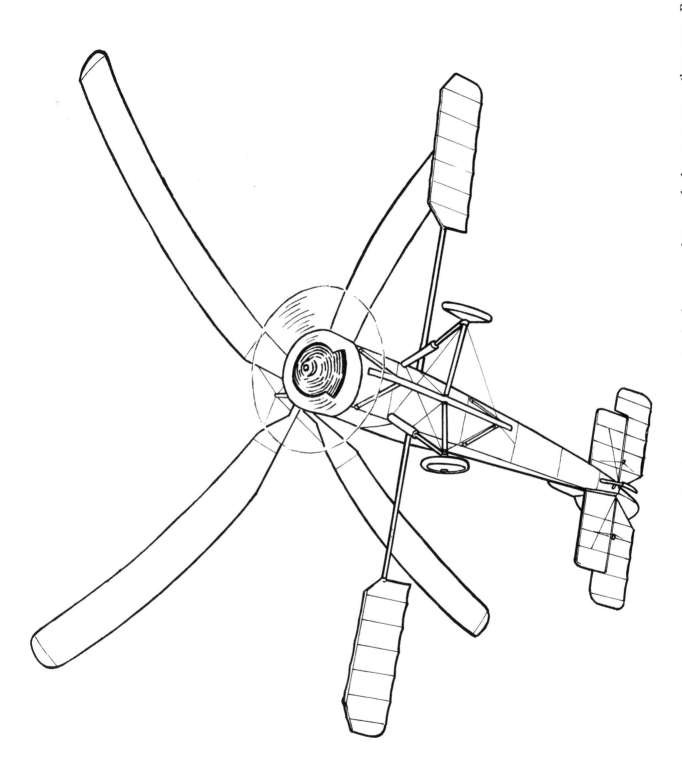

19. Cierva Autogiro, 1923–1924. A forerunner of the modern helicopter, the Cierva autogiro, designed by Juan de la Cierva, first flew in Madrid in 1923. Aircraft was colored bright yellow throughout. The rudder and wheels were white, and the nose was silver-grey. Rotor-blade diameter 36'.

20. Waco 9, 1925–1927. A popular postwar American design, the Waco 9 was used as a crop duster, barnstormer and early airliner. Aircraft was all red throughout, with white letters on wings and tail. Wingspan 29'6".

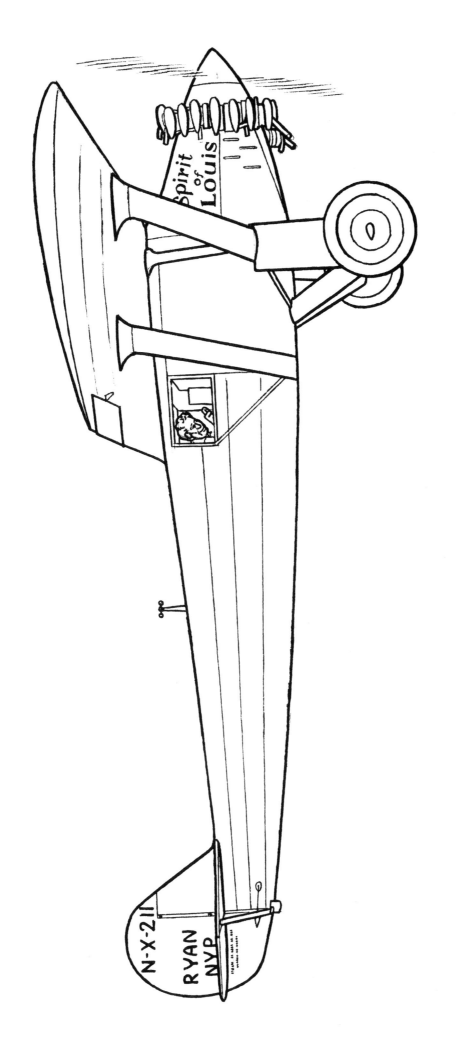

21. Ryan NYP Monoplane, 1927. This specially built plane, "The Spirit of St. Louis," was flown by Charles Lindbergh on his famed solo crossing of the Atlantic Ocean, from New York to Paris, May 20–21, 1927.

22. Aeronca C-2, 1928. An interesting little plane, the Aeronca C-2 was originally planned to be the first mass-produced popular sports plane available to everyone. The great depression put an end to this idea. Aircraft had white upper fuselage and wings. Lower fuselage, nose and tail were dark red. Stripe up leading edge of vertical tail section was white, as was lower part of rudder. Wheels were dark red. Wingspan 35'.

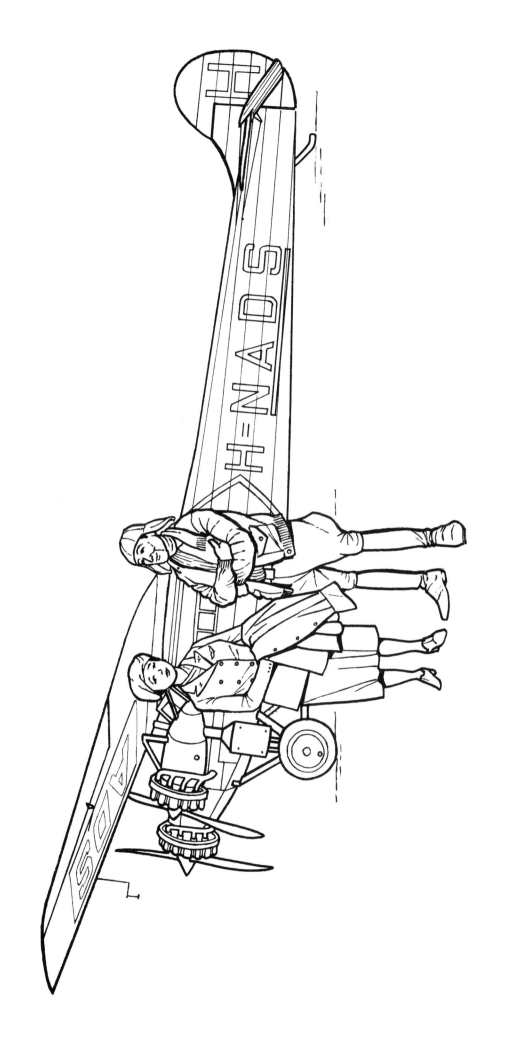

23. Fokker F.VII, 1929. The first F.VII types were put in airline service with the Dutch KLM airline as early as 1925, and the airplane was a great success. This type was used by a number of American airline companies. Aircraft had green wings with silver-grey fuselage and tail. Fuselage from pilot's cockpit back to letters was royal blue with white trim. Letters were royal blue. Wingspan 72'.

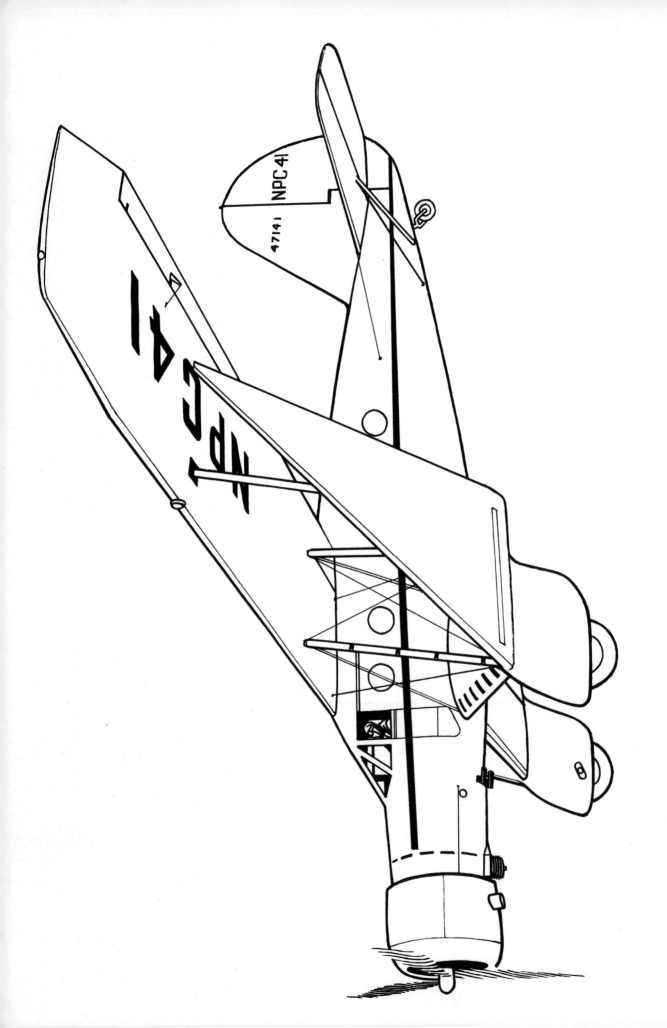

24. Bellanca Air Cruiser, 1930. One airplane of this type gave daily commuter service to business executives from Long Island to the Hudson end of Wall Street in New York City in the early 1930's. Air-craft colored pale green throughout with black striping and lettering. Wingspan 65'.

NPC 41

47141 NPC 41

NPC 41

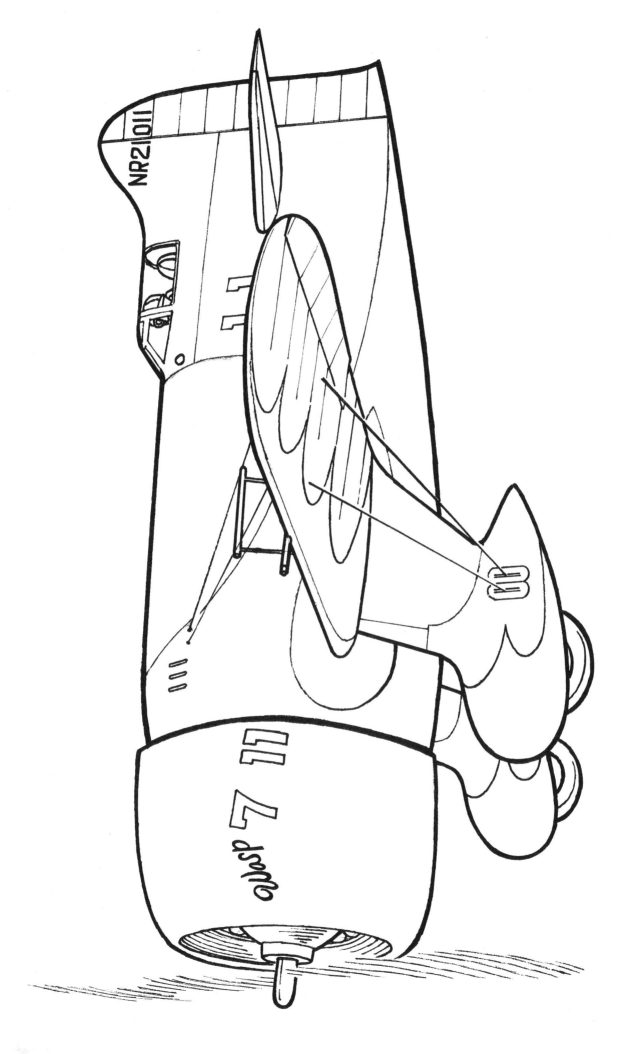

25. Gee Bee R-1, 1932. Piloted by Jimmy Doolittle, this stubby monoplane won the Thompson Trophy Air Race of 1932 with a record speed of 252 mph. Aircraft had a black nose and under fuselage; leading edge of wings and wheel spats were also black. Remainder of plane was bright yellow with black lettering on yellow areas and white lettering on nose. Wingspan 25.

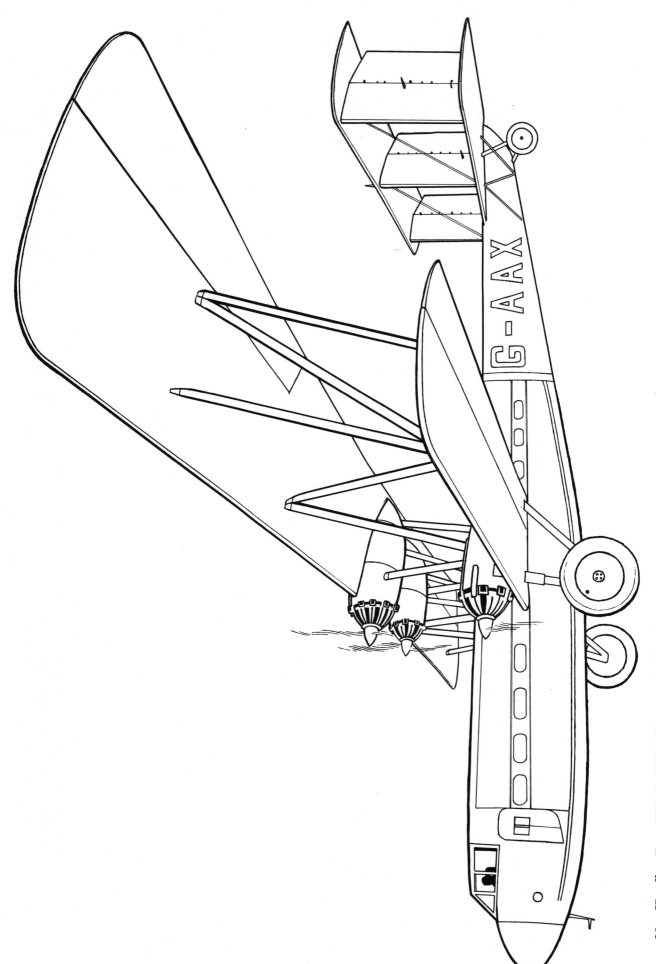

26. **Handley Page H.P.42, 1932.** This was the first four-engined passenger-carrying airplane to go into airline service—with the British Imperial Airways Company. Aircraft was silver-grey throughout, with blue lettering on fuselage. Wingspan 130'.

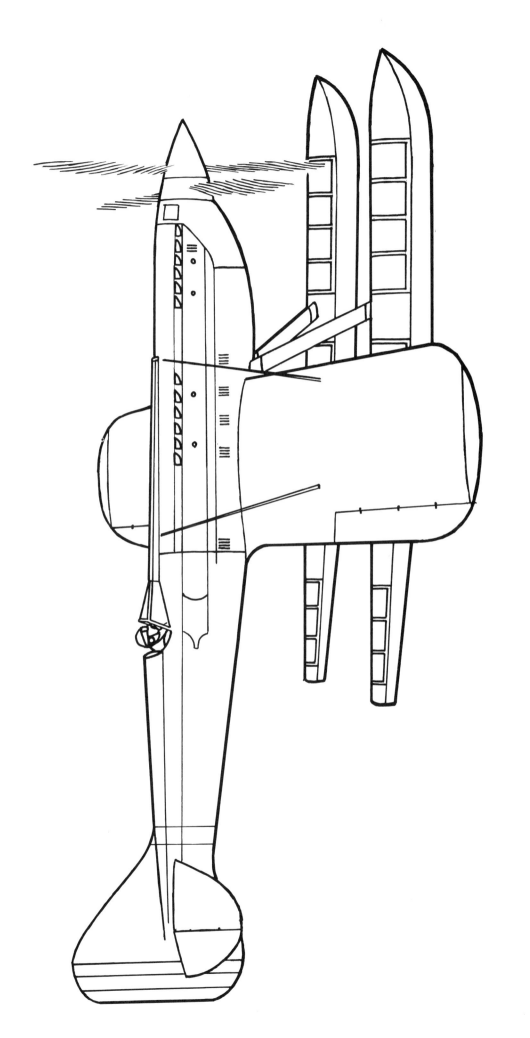

27. Macchi Castoldi MC 72, 1933. This is the Italian racer that established the world's record speed of 440 mph for piston-engined seaplanes, a record that has never been surpassed in this category. Aircraft was colored maroon throughout, with a white stripe on rear fuselage. The propeller spinner and floats were silver-grey. The rudder was striped (front to rear) green, white, red. Wings were golden yellow. Wingspan 31'9".

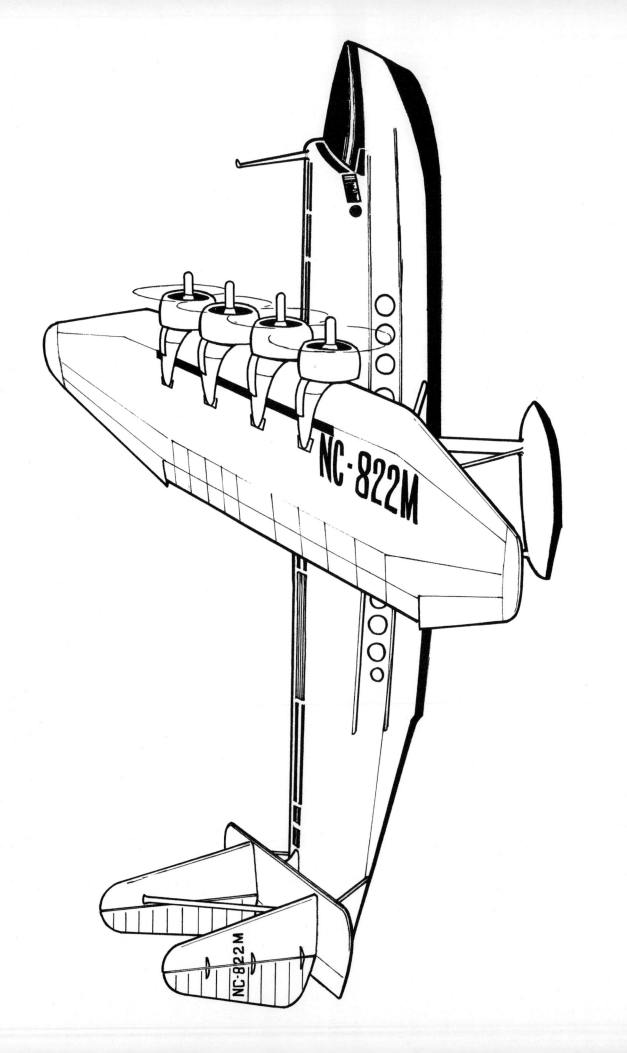

28. Sikorsky S-42, 1934. This record-breaking airplane could carry 32 passengers for 2400 miles. The S-42 was employed by Pan American Airways in 1934. Aircraft was silver-grey throughout, with black lettering. Wingspan 118'.

NC-822M

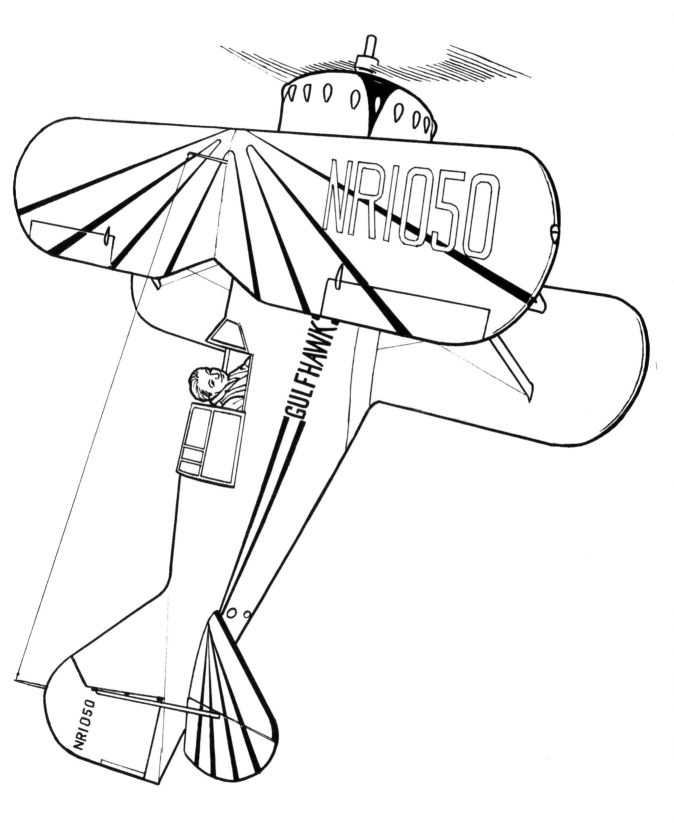

29. Grumman Gulfhawk, 1936. This little biplane was one of the most acrobatic airplanes of all time. It is now in the collection of the National Air and Space Museum, Smithsonian Institution, Washington, D.C.

Aircraft was bright orange throughout, the wings having black and white stripes. The fuselage and tail section also had black and white stripes. Lettering on the upper wing was black. Wingspan 28'6".

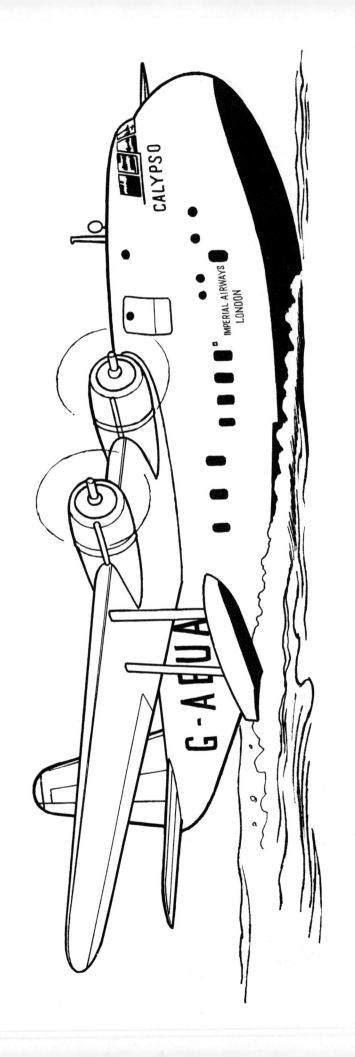

30. Short Empire Flying Boat, 1936. This British flying boat set a trans-Atlantic speed record of 15 hours, 3 minutes, in July 1937. Aircraft was colored silver-grey throughout with blue trim on engine cowlings. Wingspan 112'10".

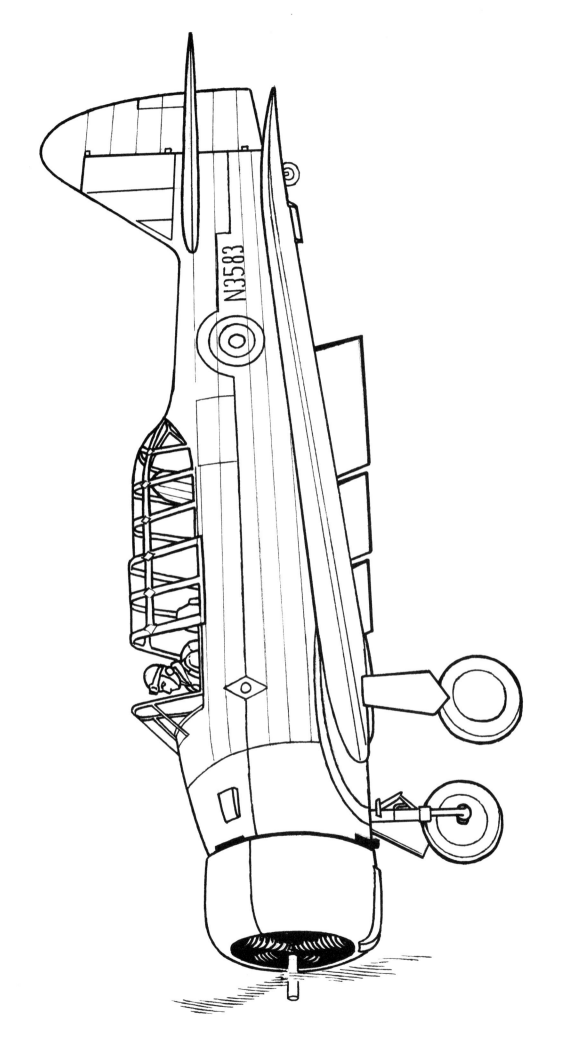

31. North American AT-6 Harvard Trainer, 1938. Perhaps the most popular and most widely used training aircraft ever designed, the AT-6 was known as the "Texan" in U.S. military service. Shown here in World War II Canadian colors, the aircraft has a fuselage the top of which is mixed green and brown camouflage, and the lower part bright yellow. Wings and tail are brown and green mixed camouflage. Roundel on fuselage (Canadian national insignia) is (outer to inner circles) blue, white, red. Stripes on tail fin are (front to rear) red, white, blue. Wingspan 43'.

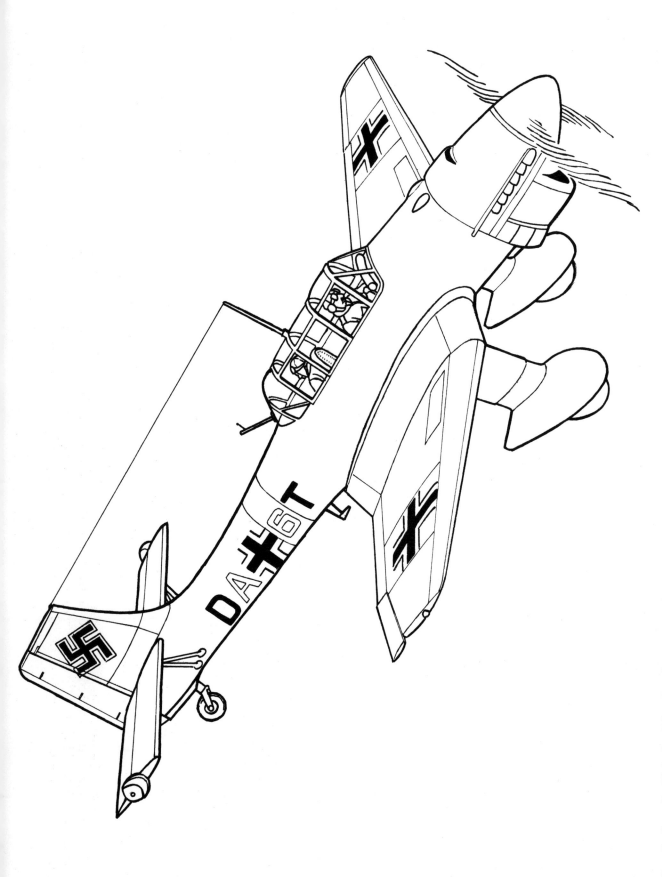

32. Junkers Ju.87 Stuka Dive Bomber, 1939. This German dive bomber, which created a sensation in the early years of World War II, was largely outclassed by the Allies later in the war, being too slow and vulnerable to fighter attack. Aircraft was dark green throughout, the nose and rudder being bright yellow. The German national insignia was the black cross and swastika with white border. Letters on fuselage are black and white. Stripe on rear part of fuselage is deep yellow. Wing tips are bright yellow. Wingspan 45'3".

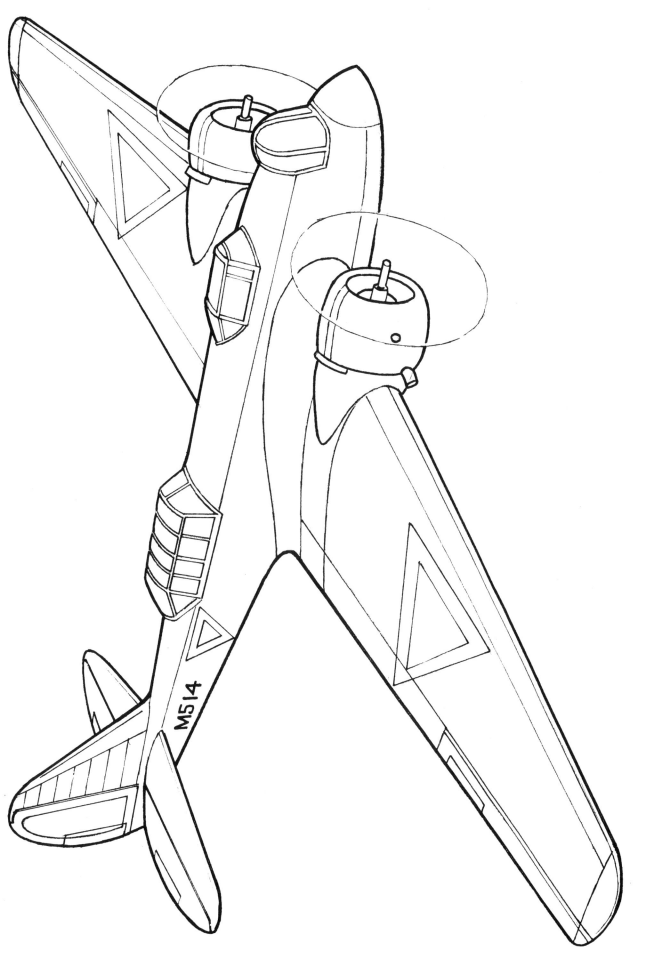

33. **Martin B-12 Bomber, 1941.** This prewar American bomber served with the U.S. Army, the Royal Thai Air Force, the Argentine Air Force and the Dutch East Indies Army in the early years of World War II. Shown here in the prewar colors of the Dutch East Indies Army, the entire aircraft is in dark green and brown camouflage throughout, the rudder orange with a black outline. The triangles on fuselage and wings (Dutch prewar national insignia) are orange with a black border. Wingspan 70'2".

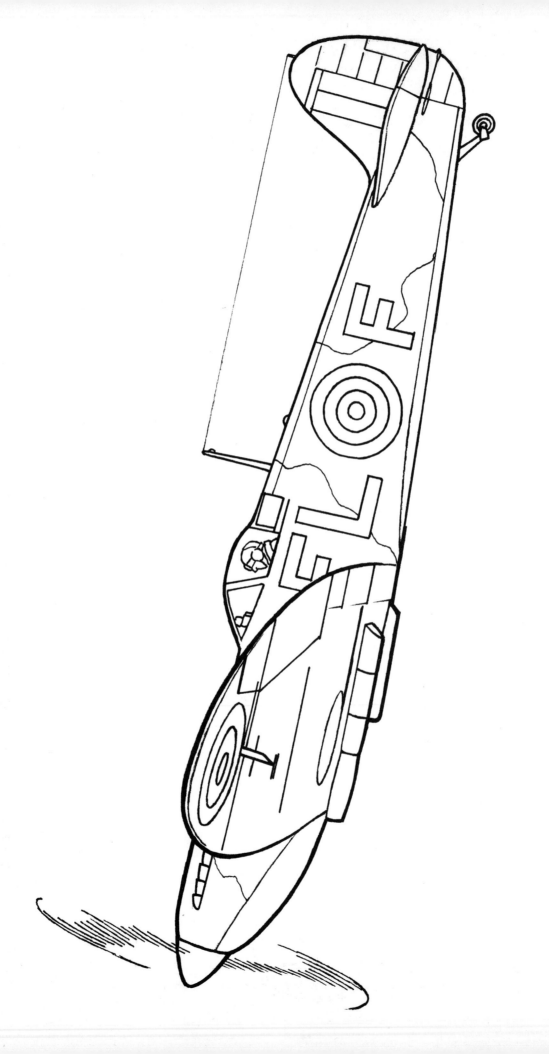

34. Supermarine Spitfire, 1940. The most famous fighter plane of the RAF during World War II, the Spitfire was largely responsible for the German defeat in the Battle of Britain of 1940. Aircraft is in mixed green and brown camouflage throughout, the undersides pale sky blue. Lettering on fuselage is white. Propeller spinner is bright blue. Roundel on fuselage (British national insignia) is (outer to inner) yellow, blue, white, red. Roundel on wing is (outer to inner) blue, white, red. Wingspan 36'10".

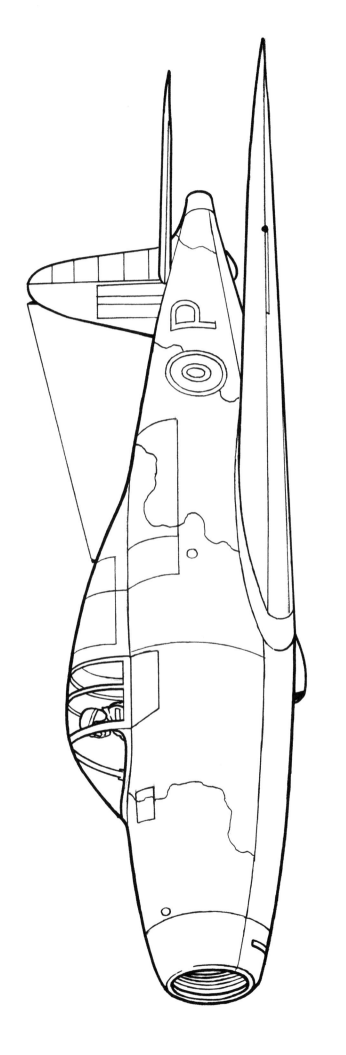

35. Gloster E.28, 1941. Britain's first jet-propelled aircraft. First flew in May of 1941. Aircraft is colored throughout in green and brown mixed camouflage. Under side of entire aircraft is pale sky blue. Stripes on tail fin are (front to back) red, white, blue. Letter on fuselage is yellow. Roundel on fuselage is (outer to inner) yellow, blue, white, red. Wingspan 43'.

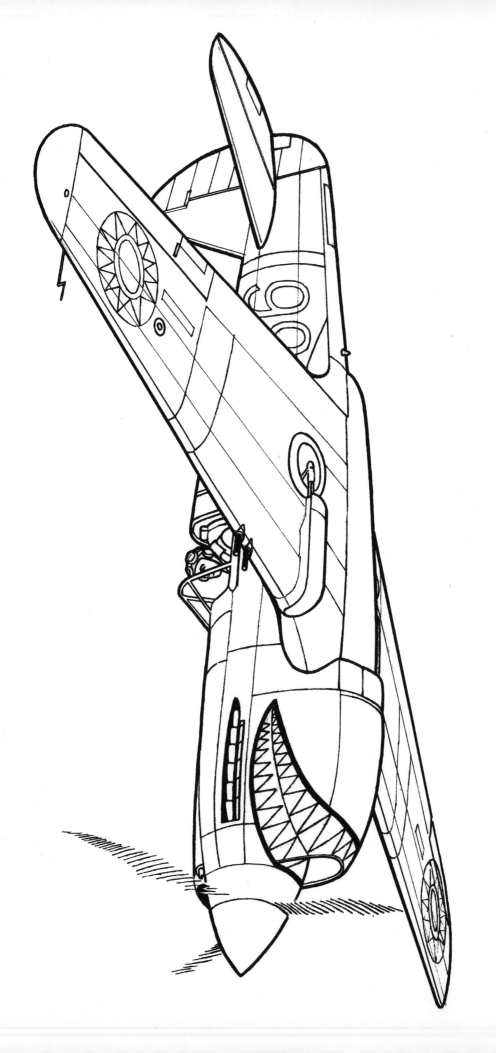

36. Curtiss P-40, 1942. This American fighter plane was used by the U.S. Army, RAF, Soviet Air Force and Nationalist Chinese Air Force among others during World War II. Shown in Chinese Nationalist colors as flown by the American Volunteer Group (Flying Tigers), the aircraft is in mixed brown and green camouflage throughout, the undersides of the entire airplane being white. The teeth on the nose are white, and the inner mouth red. Letters and stripe on fuselage are white, and Chinese insignia is a white star within a blue circle with a blue stripe enclosing a white center. Wingspan 37'4".

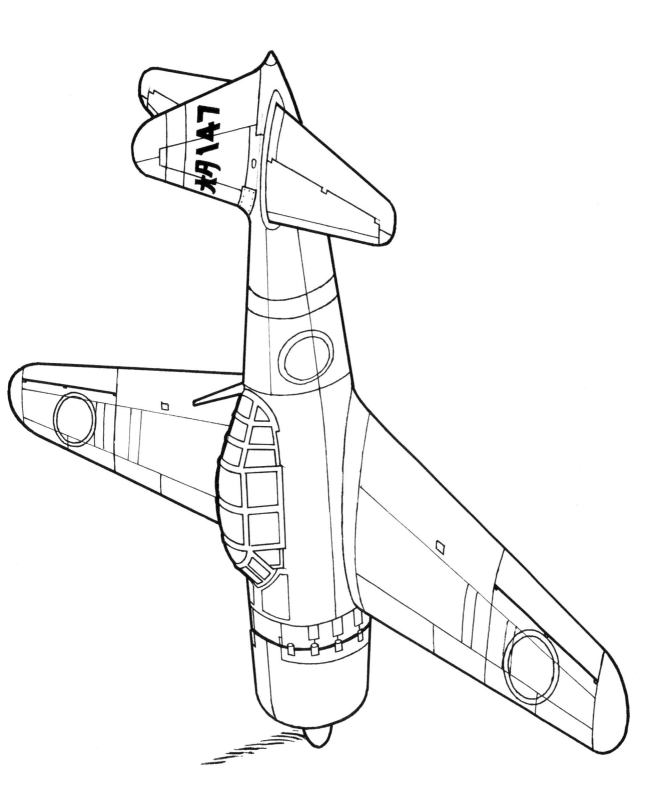

37. Mitsubishi Zero Fighter, 1941–1943. This Japanese fighter plane, vastly underrated by the Americans at the outbreak of the Pacific war, was a highly maneuverable aircraft and formed the backbone of the Japanese pursuit service during World War II. Aircraft colored medium green throughout, propeller spinner was yellow. Fuselage band was white, and Japanese national insignia on fuselage and wings was a red ball with a white outline. Band across tail fin and rudder was yellow. Wingspan 39′5″.

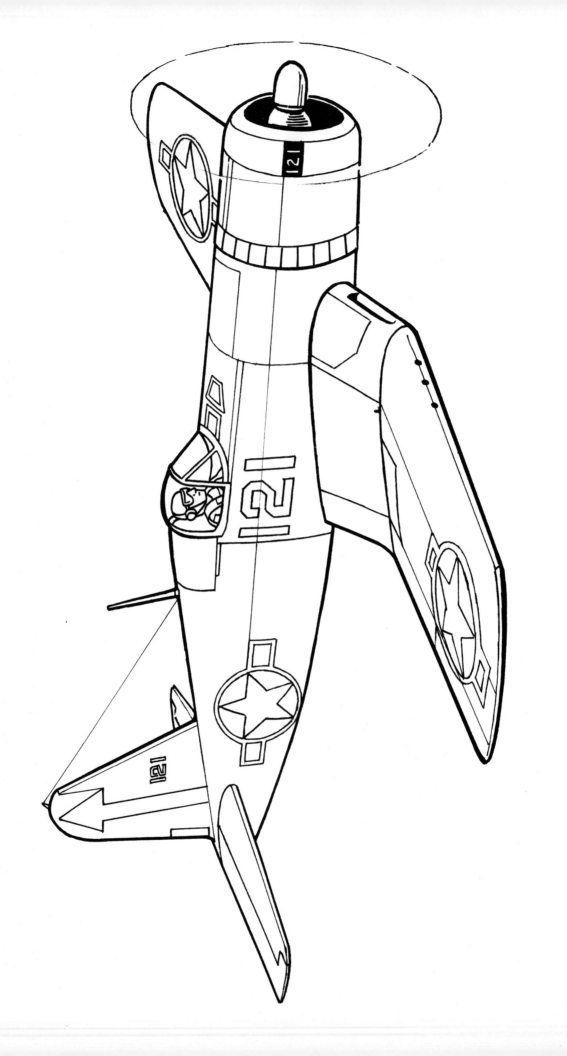

38. Vought F4U-1 Corsair, 1944. This U.S. Navy and Marine Corps fighter plane arrived in the Southwest Pacific in 1943 and immediately began to turn the tide of aerial combat in favor of the Americans. The Corsair was able to outclass the formidable Japanese Zero in combat. Aircraft is grey-blue throughout; lettering on fuselage and arrow on tail white, as is front of cowling on nose. U.S. insignia on fuselage and wings, white star and side bars within black circle and borders. Wingspan 40'11".

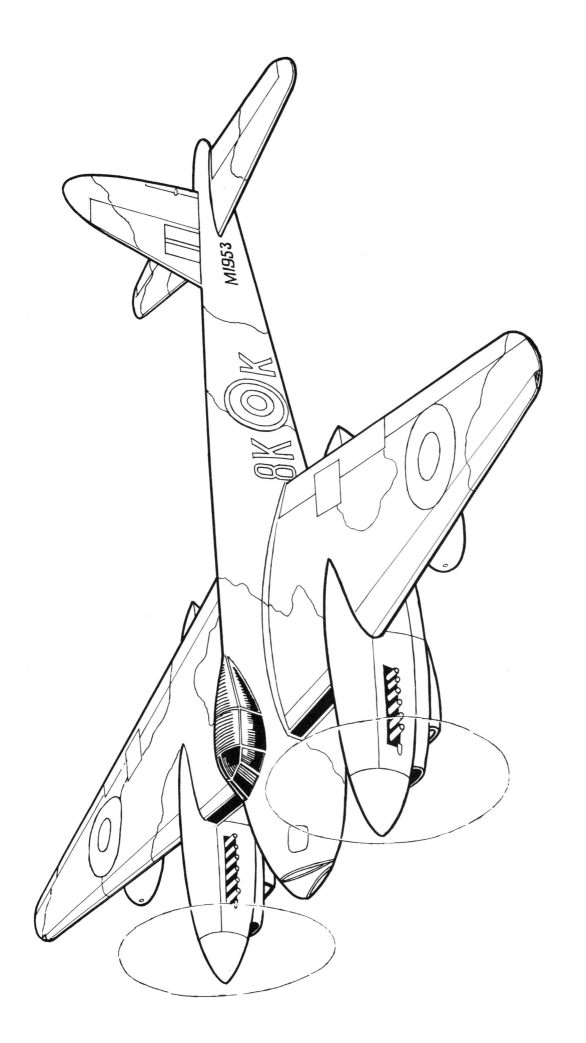

39. De Havilland Mosquito, 1944-1945. This speedy British bomber was so versatile that it also served the RAF as a night fighter and a high-speed reconnaissance plane. Nearly eight thousand Mosquitos were built during World War II. Aircraft pale green and brown mixed camouflage throughout. Propeller spinners were light blue. Lettering on fuselage was red. Wing roundels (British national insignia) were (outer to inner) blue and red. Fuselage roundel was (outer to inner) yellow, blue, white, red. Stripes on tail fin were (front to rear) red, white, blue. Wingspan 54′2″.

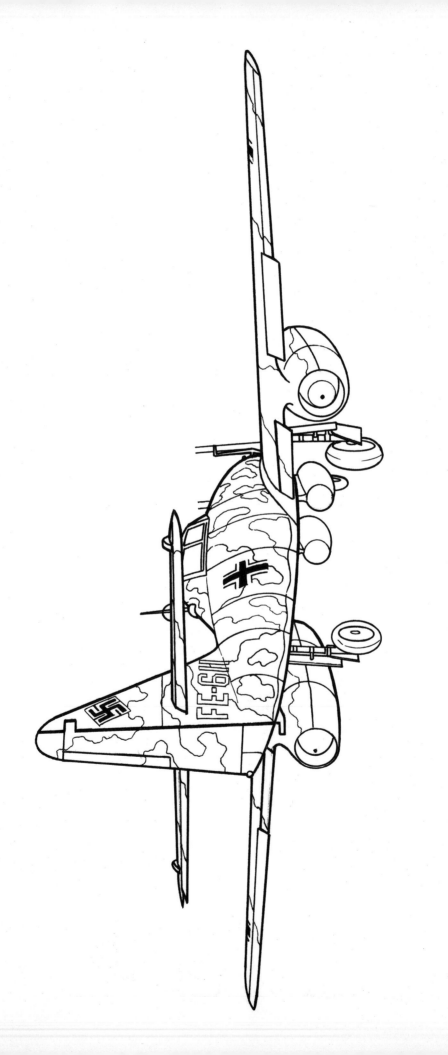

40. Messerschmitt Me. 262, 1945. The world's first fully operational jet fighter, the Me. 262 had a maximum speed of over 500 mph. Aircraft was a mottled deep green and brown throughout. Lettering on tail section was white. Wingspan 41'2".

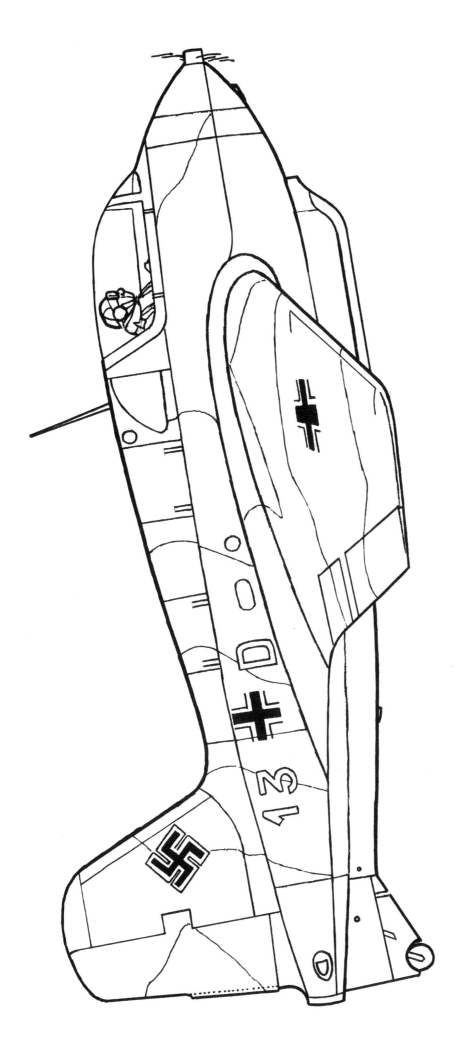

41. Messerschmitt Me. 163, 1945. The world's first operational rocket-powered fighter, the Me. 163 had a phenomenal ability to climb and a top speed of about 550 mph. It was a very dangerous airplane to fly. Aircraft was a mottled light and dark blue green throughout, the undersides were light sky-blue. Lettering on fuselage was yellow, as was the nose. Wingspan 32'2".